A Pathway to an Abundant Life
Christian Coping Skills

Acknowledgments

I would like to acknowledge my husband, Richard, and our children, Sharon, Susan and Steven for their support. You are all an inspiration to me.

Dedication

I dedicate this book to my Grandchildren: Justin, Hailey, Makayla, Joey, Jake, Carter and Henry. I wish each of you an abundant life. I love you all so much. Thank you for being the person God created you to be.

About the Author

Karen Espeland has a Master's degree in Nursing and has spent her professional career in healthcare and related fields. She has been a nurse in varied areas of nursing, a nursing professor for over 20 years, and Director of Nurses at an inpatient addiction treatment facility. Her research and publications related to mental health, addiction, and workplace issues have been published and recognized in many professional journals in the United States and internationally. Throughout her life, she has also been active in her Christian faith, teaching in her church and presenting a Christian Care Giving course to Caregivers. It is her hope that through this book, the reader will increase their understanding and coping skills to be able to more fully appreciate the abundant life that they can have as a Christian.

TABLE OF CONTENTS

Surviving Life's Greatest Challenges

Developing a Forgiving Approach to Life

Communication with Self and Others

Healthy Living

Living a Christian Lifestyle

Following Jesus

INTRODUCTION

This book provides guidance, encouragement, reassurance and comfort as we journey through life, based on scripture from the Bible. Reading this book enables us to have the opportunity to come closer to being the person God intended us to be.
Jesus came so that we can live more abundantly. *"I came that they may have and enjoy life, and have it in abundance."* (John 10:10b AMP). He wanted us to have a quality life, even exceeding what we are currently experiencing. We frequently think abundance is having money, possessions, prestige, popularity or friends and that is what we seek. Each day we work harder and harder to achieve these goals yet end up feeling empty.

"A Pathway to an Abundant Life-Christian Coping Skills" provides insight into how to get through the tough times and re-establish a relationship with God and others. When we go through change and difficulties in our life the mind can become our worst enemy. Our thoughts focus on worries, fear, and negative thoughts. Allowing our mind to remain on this can only compound our difficulties. Sometimes we feel so distraught by something that has happened that we cannot find any assets in ourselves.

This book was written because there is very little concise informative literature available on the wonderful abundant life God wants us to have. He does not want us to just stay the way we are. He wants us to have a life free of stress and worry, yet one in which we find happiness by helping others.

—

"A Pathway to an Abundant Life-Christian Coping Skills" is an empowering resource for those:

- Experiencing changes in their life
- Trying to find a purpose in life
- Facing choices in a career
- Developing a relationship with God
- Focusing on bad decisions or a failure in life
- Lacking resources to pursue dreams
- Ruminating on negative thoughts
- Struggling to forgive someone
- Seeking suggestions on healthy living
- Establishing or questioning Christian values

Developing an Abundant Life

Use the Gifts and Talents God Has Given You

Each of us has been given gifts from God. *"Do not neglect the gift that is in you, which was given to you through prophecy when the elders laid their hands on you."* (1 Timothy 4:14 ISV) There is an old saying, "God did not make junk." Periodically we may compare ourselves to others, perhaps thinking that their gifts/talents are better than ours. Some of us wish we would have different gifts. God made each of us special. He made each and every one of us to fulfill our God-given, divine purpose. We have just the talents we need. Some of us lack the faith to believe that God has a tremendous future in mind for us. All we need to do is pray for guidance to use and not neglect our gifts. Ask God his plan for your life, to show you the gifts he has given you. Let's not hide those gifts. The verse from the children's hymn "This little light of mine, I'm going to let it shine" is an example of how God wants us to use our gifts to His glory.

Be a Lifelong Learner

We sometimes set limitations in our minds about what we can achieve. Comments such as "I might as well accept who I am and be content" drastically inhibit our potential for growth. Sometimes our inner urge to grow is inhibited by the fear we cannot succeed. At these times we need to reach out for encouragement from our family, friends and our Best Friend, God. God loves us just the way we are but refuses to leave us that way. God wants us to steadily grow, especially in our knowledge of him. Our desire to grow, to make a place for ourselves in the world, is healthy and necessary to our existence. The inner drive to move ahead, try a new approach to a problem, seek a career, or to learn a new hobby, are evidence of God's Spirituality within us. *"That you may walk (live and conduct yourselves) in a manner worthy of the Lord, fully pleasing to Him and desiring to please Him in all things, bearing fruit in every good work and steadily growing and increasing in and by the knowledge of God with fuller, deeper, and clearer insight, acquaintance, and recognition."* (Colossians 1:10 AMP)

Find a Purpose

God has a purpose in life for each of us. We are one of a kind. Questions to ask ourselves to help find a purpose include: "What is my passion?" "What excites me?" "What do I think is God's purpose for my life?" Each day we should ask God to help us find a purpose for the day. When we have clear, exciting goals and ideals, we feel happier about ourselves and our world. Finding our passion creates energy and gives us purpose. It is wonderful to know that God loves us and has unique plans for each of us. *"Many are the plans in a person's heart, but it is the Lord's purpose that prevails."* (Proverbs 19:21 NIV) Each day in prayer we must ask God to help us you find our purpose for that day and our lives.

Identify Problems/Challenges

Each day will bring some type of challenge. Do not wish your problems and challenges away. They are an inevitable part of life. When we are facing a situation that seems like it is impossible to solve, ask God for guidance. God has promised to always be there for us. *"But if any of you lacks wisdom, he should ask God, who gives generously to all without finding fault, and it will be given to him. But when he asks, he must believe and not doubt, because he who doubts is like a wave of the sea, blown and tossed by the wind."* (James 1:5-6 NIV) God is faithful to provide input. Sometimes this may be through counseling, praying, and fellowship with fellow Christian friends, devotional books or the Bible. Keep a positive look on life. Look at things in a new way, seeing problems as opportunities.

Solve Problems

Problems are an inevitable part of life. Recognizing the type of problems we face can help us effectively deal with them.

Problems can be separated into two types:
- Those that can be solved with a positive attitude.
- Those that can never be solved by thinking or worrying about them.

The following are effective steps we can take to solve a problem:
- Identify the problem.
- Assess your desire to solve the problem. Running away, ignoring problems, or denying that they exist will usually not help.
- Ask God for guidance in solving the problem.
- Ask yourself, "How would God solve this problem?"
- Ask for advice from people you respect.
- Develop a plan to solve the problem.
- Write down possible solutions.
- Choose the best solution.
- Stay focused. Don't quit trying to solve the problem. If the first solution doesn't work, pick the second solution. When we solve a problem, our confidence will grow the next time a problem occurs.

People like to associate with people who constructively solve problems instead of complaining about them.

"But those who hope in the Lord will renew their strength. They will soar on wings like eagles; they will run and not grow weary, they will walk and not be faint." (Isaiah 40:31 NIV) There is no problem that cannot be solved; God is right beside us guiding us each and every step through the problem-solving process.

Have Perseverance

Is there anything in life that we are afraid to try because we do not think we can? Sometimes we feel we don't have enough education or intellect. But, after developing a worthwhile goal, keep on striving toward it. Pray to God for His guidance. Step back and try a new approach if it doesn't work out right away, but do not give up. Time, patience, confidence, perseverance and trust in God will help you reach the goal. *"For I can do everything with the help of Christ who gives me the strength I need."* (Philippians 4:13 NLT)

Understand Fame and Fortune

Being famous and having a fortune may be more dangerous for the Christian than persecution. Many Christians would like to be famous and rich. This is OK unless it weakens our relationship with God. Sometimes in order to be well known and liked by others, we are more interested in what others think and less focused on what God thinks. Even when we are not famous or rich we are to be content. *"I am not saying this because I am in need, for I have learned to be content whatever the circumstances."* (Philippians 4:11 NIV)

—

Use Money Wisely

Decide to exercise self-control when deciding how to use money. Having material possessions does not mean that we will be happy or have a great life. For example, having a house does not mean we have a home. *"Stay away from the love of money; be satisfied with what you have"* (Hebrews 13:5 a NLT)

It is not how much we make, but how much we spend that determines how much money we have. Spending excess amounts of money early in life can haunt us for years to come.

Keep a Good Reputation

A good reputation, not money or good looks, is one of our greatest assets. *"Choose a good reputation over great riches, for being held in high esteem is better than having silver or gold"*. (Proverbs 22:1 NLT) A good reputation is not something that is achieved overnight. It's the product of persistent action over time. It is much easier to keep a good reputation than rebuild a reputation; however, over time we can re-establish our good name. We should live our lives in such a way that our actions will speak louder than words.

Be Honest

Honesty is always the best policy. *"Honesty guides good people; dishonesty destroys treacherous people."* (Proverbs 11:3 NLT) Nothing creates distrust like lying, even if it's over something considered immaterial.

Honesty is a direct reflection of inner character. Our actions are a reflection of our faith. Those who are honest and always tell the truth have a precious possession – a clear conscience.

Those who always tell the truth have the respect of others. They are trusted. Honesty is considered a characteristic that friends, family, teachers and employers consider admirable. When you are faithful and honest, it shows. *"Whoever can be trusted with very little can also be trusted with much, and whoever is dishonest with very little will also be dishonest with much."* (Luke 16:10 NIV)

Preparing for Life's Inevitable Challenges

Our Burdens

Jesus understands the burdens we carry because He, too, had burdens when He was on Earth. Psalm 55 gives us direction on how to cope with our burdens. *"Cast your cares on the Lord and he will sustain you; he will never let the righteous fall."* (Psalm 55:22 NIV) Jesus shares our burdens. *"Come to me, all you who are weary and burdened, and I will give you rest. Take my yoke upon you and learn from me, for I am gentle and humble in heart, and you will find rest for your souls. For my yoke is easy and my burden is light."* (Matthew 11: 28-30 NIV) Give your burdens to Him; Jesus is right beside us helping us struggle with our burdens. Ask God to give you strength, to bear your burdens.

We can get tired of burdens in life, but knowing that one day we will be with Jesus in Heaven should help us handle the burdens of Earth. Keep focused on eternity. *"So we don't look at the troubles we can see now; rather, we fix our gaze on things that cannot be seen. For the things we see now will soon be gone, but the things we cannot see will last forever."* (2 Corinthians 4: 18 NLT)

Others' Burdens

Look for ways to help others. Offer financial assistance, give support in a crisis or offer a kind word, smile and acknowledge those who are struggling in life. Jesus said that when we reach out to help another, we are reaching out to the Lord. *"And he will answer, 'I tell you the truth, when you refused to help the least of these my brothers and sisters, you were refusing to help me.'"* (Matthew 25:45 NLT)

A proven way to beat depression, loneliness or the blahs is to reach out to others. Happiness comes as we give the gift of ourselves to others. When we put behind us the stresses caused by life and offer our help to someone in need, we have lightened our load. We will still return to the same worries and frustrations as before, but we will come to them with renewed energy and a sense of gratitude for all that we have been given, and a heightened awareness of the steady and loving presence of God in our lives.

Set Boundaries

"Carry each other's burdens, and in this way you will fulfill the law of Christ..... for each one should carry his own load." (Galatians 6:2, 5 NIV) These verses are in the same chapter, but contradict each other. Verse 2 asks us to bear another's burdens, while Verse 5 asks us to let others carry their own load.

A burden can be like trying to carry several cement blocks that are too heavy for anyone. We should offer to help people who have a burden, especially in a crisis.

But, a load can be like a backpack. If people ask for help with a load that can easily be carried, we should say "no." It is important that we don't enable people or do for people what they can do for themselves. These people need encouragement in taking responsibility for themselves.

It is also important to set priorities of how we use your time. It is OK to set boundaries and not commit to more than we can handle. Say "No" to excessive demands and "Yes" to time for yourself and time with God.

Seek Help in a Crisis

Crisis is an inevitable part of life. Some will be caused by natural disaster such as earthquake, hurricane or some other large magnitude act of nature beyond our control. Some will be caused by more personal experiences such as illness, date rape, or another difficult experience. No matter the crisis, praying to God for comfort and guidance will help us work through it. He will walk beside us. *"Never will I leave you; never will I forsake you."* (Hebrews 13:5 NIV). A crisis can be traumatic and professional help from a counselor or a pastor may be needed.

Receive Encouragement

When we experience a crisis, we also need to reach out to people who support us, make good decisions and use positive coping skills. Seeking encouragement makes many of us feel uncomfortable. Some of us grew up feeling that we needed to be independent and not ask others for support or assistance. Don't go it alone. We need to talk to our trusted family and close friends about our problems. They very well may offer a different perspective to the situation, provide a listening ear and support us during this difficult time.

We need to find individuals who can be a source of encouragement. This is similar to friendship but encouragement is more complex. It means finding someone and being there for one another. Encouragers need to bring out the best in each other, yet sometimes help look at a problem from a different perspective. This is a positive relationship in which we can be who we are rather than whom others expect us to be. Christians have been encouraging each other since Biblical times. *"Your love has given me great joy and encouragement, because you, brother, have refreshed the hearts of the saints."* (Philemon 1:7 NIV)

A strong sense of community support helps us survive tough situations. Joining a congregation enables us to be in a community of believers that provides us support and encouragement. Sometimes we need to try different types of congregations to find the one that best meets our needs.

—

Be an Encourager

Giving encouragement to others is also difficult for some of us. The Apostle Paul exhorted the church in the town of Thessalonica to be encouragers. *"Therefore encourage one another and build each other up, just as in fact you are doing."* (1Thessalonians 5:11 NIV)

Encouragers listen and are sounding boards for us. Listening is key to being encouragers, but they also accept and ask questions, offering no answers. Encouragers also need to show respect for the feelings and thoughts of others.

Surviving a Loss

The Apostle Paul had a faith-filled perspective on loss. *"What is more, I consider everything a loss compared to the surpassing greatness of knowing Christ Jesus my Lord, for whose sake I have lost all things."* (Philippians 3:8a NIV). Sometimes we experience great loss in our life, perhaps the loss of a relationship or death of a loved one. This was true for the author of the hymn, "What a Friend we have in Jesus." His fiancé died the night before their wedding. From this tragedy he wrote the following beautiful words. Prayer was his answer to overcoming his grief.

Read the words slowly:

What a Friend we have in Jesus, all our sins and griefs to bear!
What a privilege to carry everything to God in prayer!

___

19

O what peace we often forfeit, O what needless pain we bear,
All because we do not carry everything to God in prayer.

Have we trials and temptations? Is there trouble anywhere?
We should never be discouraged; take it to the Lord in prayer.
Can we find a friend so faithful who will all our sorrows share?
Jesus knows our every weakness; take it to the Lord in prayer.

Are we weak and heavy laden, cumbered with a load of care?
Precious Savior, still our refuge, take it to the Lord in prayer.
Do your friends despise, forsake you? Take it to the Lord in prayer!
In His arms He'll take and shield you; you will find a solace there.

Blessed Savior, Thou hast promised Thou wilt all our burdens bear
May we ever, Lord, be bringing all to Thee in earnest prayer.
Soon in glory bright unclouded there will be no need for prayer
Rapture, praise and endless worship will be our sweet portion there

Surviving loss is never easy. It is one of the hardest events our lives. This is the time we need to surround ourselves with encouraging supportive people to help share the memories of our loss. If we do not have the support we need, we should seek out a counselor.

Tears are healthy, so let them come freely. If we feel angry, we need to express it, in a healthy way that does not cause harm to us or someone else. It is OK to feel angry, even if it is at God. Expressing anger will help it fade with time. If we feel hopeless, it is because we are realizing that things are not in our own control. This is when faith, prayer and a belief in God are helpful. Talking to our Pastor will also help.

Healing from loss may take a year or longer. There is an old saying, "Time heals all things." Whatever the loss, things may not be the same again, but we need to hold on to the hope that our lives once again will be filled with joy and happiness.

Listen With Your Heart

Listen with your heart. One of the greatest desires of the human heart is to have someone genuinely listen. Listening means paying attention to what a person is saying, acknowledging feelings, holding back on what we have to say, avoiding interruption and controlling the urge to give advice. Our physical presence and desire to listen without judging are critical helping tools. We shouldn't worry so much about what to say. Instead, we should just concentrate on listening to the words that are being shared.

The first characteristic of a good listener is a desire to listen. People can readily detect a superficial desire to listen. To be a good listener we must want to hear what is being said. The second characteristic of a good listener is patience. If we are in a hurry and anxious for the person to finish talking, that impatience will be communicated. *"My dear brothers and sisters, take note of this: Everyone should be quick to listen, slow to speak."*(James 1:19 NIV) Many times we have the answers to our situations, but we need someone to patiently listen as we express our feelings. We need to be good listeners but also find someone who can genuinely listen to us.

Comfort Others as God Comforts Us

God is available to comfort us. *"Blessed be the God and Father of our Lord Jesus, the Messiah! He is our merciful Father and the God of all comfort, who comforts us in all our suffering, so that we may be able to comfort others in all their suffering, as we ourselves are being comforted by God."* (2 Corinthians 1:3-4 ISV)

In other words, since we are comforted by God in our difficult times, we should also comfort others in their difficulties, whether they are brokenhearted from a death, broken relationship, loss of job, failing grades, strained relationships with teachers and/or parents or other traumatic events. We are asked to be messengers of God's love.

Surviving Life's Greatest Challenges

Build on Failure

Failure is only a discovery. If something does not work out in our lives we shouldn't beat ourselves up or dwell on it. Don't give up. Build on it. Everyone fails. In the Bible, some of the greatest leaders, including Moses, David, Peter and Paul, suffered failures. Perhaps the biggest failure is not trying something for fear of failure.

Giving some thought to our failures is not necessarily a bad thing – especially if doing so moves us to make improvements. However, prolonged and unrelenting self-criticism is harmful and counterproductive. *"An anxious heart weighs a man down, but a kind word cheers him up."* (Proverbs 12:25 NIV) Successful people use failures as an opportunity to grow, while those who lack success allow failures to overwhelm them and leave them discouraged and dejected. We must avoid taking ourselves too seriously. If we feel discouraged, we should turn our attention toward something that we do well, such as a hobby or a sport or doing something for others.

Grow From Adversity

Some challenges may look like adversity. We have a choice. We can use adversity and struggles for growth or allow them to overwhelm us and leave us discouraged and dejected. Adversity may come from past experiences. It has been said, "It doesn't matter where you are coming from; all that really matters is where you are going."

Instead of asking, "Why Me?" say, "Even though this is a difficult situation, what can I learn from it." "How can I benefit from this challenge or adversity?" The test we must pass on the path to accomplishing anything worthwhile is the definition of adversity. We grow closer to God when we experience adversity. We must ask God for the faith to keep going and keep believing that He has a wonderful plan for us. Have the courage and faith to venture out and try again. Trust God to help take the first step.

President Lincoln never let adversity wear him down.   Few people have had as much adversity as he did:

- His mother died when he was nine.
- He was rejected by his first love.
- His first business ended in bankruptcy.
- He was defeated the first time he ran for office.
- He served only one term in Congress because he was unpopular.

After leaving Congress, Lincoln told a friend, "I will get ready, my time will come." *"In all this you greatly rejoice, though now for a little while you may have had to suffer grief in all kinds of trials. These have come so that the proven genuineness of your faith – of greater worth than gold, which perishes even though refined by fire – may result in praise, glory and honor when Jesus Christ is revealed."* (1 Peter 1:6, 7 NIV)

——

When we experience adversity, we need to remember that our day is coming. God knows what has happened in the world, and sooner than we thought possible, He will bless us.

Accept What We Cannot Control

We have minimal control over some of the events that we experience. A relationship may break up, we may experience illness, a friend may reject or betray us or a goal may be crushed. In times like this we need to turn to those who support us and to our Best Friend, Jesus. We need to let go of things we cannot control, whether it's places, experiences, or people (such as our friends moving away). *"How precious is your unfailing love, O God! All humanity finds shelter in the shadow of your wings."* (Psalm 36:7 NLT)

Leave the Past Behind

Letting go of the old requires patience, persistence and strength. Leaving behind things we love may cause us temporary sadness, but it also provides us opportunity for growth that we may not have thought about. Moving to a new city or leaving for college can be stressful. Instead of dreading this, it's a time to reflect on the good times, appreciate what we have gained from the past and know that our life is fuller for these situations. They push us beyond ourselves to a deeper understanding of others and ourselves. *"Forget the former things; do not dwell on the past. See, I am doing a new thing! Now it springs up; do you not perceive it? I am making a way in the desert and streams in the*

25

wasteland." (Isaiah 43:18-19 NIV)

When life does not go as we expected or we make a mistake, we may want to blame others or our past for our moods, lack of accountability or bad habits. Certainly, people in the present or the past may contribute to the way we feel or actions we may take, but ultimately we are responsible. We shouldn't make excuses, instead be accountable, no matter how terrible we perceive life to be.

Cope with Change

We can be thankful for the promise that our God does not change. He is always the same. *"I the Lord do not change."* (Malachi 3:6 NIV) Change is an inevitable part of our life here on Earth. No matter how predictable and stable our life is, we all need to cope and adjust. Change is always occurring, yet when it happens we can be in turmoil and wonder, "Why did this have to happen?" The only thing constant in life is change. People change and situations change. This can happen slowly or quickly or be minor or major. Sometimes dealing with it is relatively easy, while other times it's a painful process. A very real kind of loss occurs when there is change.

With the pain can come questions like, "Why must I go through this?" The Bible tells us that everything in life will change except the word of the Lord. *"All people are like grass, and all their faithfulness is like the flowers of the field. The grass withers and the flowers fall...but the word of*

26

our God endures forever." (Isaiah 40:6-8 NIV) We cannot always control change, so when it comes, cherish the memories of the past and focus on the positive aspects of the change.

Look for the comfort in this Serenity Prayer by Reinhold Niebuhr:

> God grant me the Serenity to accept the things I cannot change.
> The courage to change the things I can, and the wisdom to know the difference.
> Living one day at a time;
> Enjoying one moment at a time;
> Accepting hardship as the pathway to peace.
>
> Taking, as He (Jesus) did, this sinful world as it is, not as I would have it;
> Trusting that He (Jesus) will make all things right if I surrender to His will;
> That I may be reasonably happy in this life, And supremely happy with Him forever in the next.

Developing a Forgiving Approach to Life

Practice Forgiveness

Forgiveness is when a person who has been hurt or insulted gives up the desire to seek revenge and wants to reconcile differences. Forgiving others is not for their benefit, it is for us. Paul writes, *"Be kind to each other, tenderhearted, forgiving one another, just as God through Christ has forgiven you."* (Ephesians 4:32 NLT). A key factor in our ability to forgive ourselves and others is determined by the closeness we feel to God. Forgiveness does not mean we have to forget or condone behavior. It does not mean we have to accept hurtful behavior or allow it to continue. Often forgiveness must happen daily. It is not something we can do once. People can be self-centered, vengeful, heartless, sadistic, vicious and mean. We need to forgive them anyway. Sometimes we want revenge because we think that will stop the hurt. But that is not our responsibility. God never encourages us to get revenge. Rather, He wants us to be an example for others of a forgiving person. Be the one to spread forgiveness and joy. We should pray for those who have wronged us, instead of criticizing or not forgiving them. *"But I tell you who hear me: Love your enemies, do good to those who hate you, bless those who curse you, pray for those who mistreat you."* (Luke 6:27-28 NIV) Truly forgiving someone means we pray for them, do good deeds for them, and love them. It is difficult to hold a grudge when you are praying for someone. Avoiding forgiving others can have consequences not only on our relationships and health, but also on our spirituality.

Forgive Yourself, Too

Forgiving yourself is instrumental to maintaining spiritual wellness. Sometimes we feel so badly about what we have done in the past, or for not meeting the expectations of others and ourselves that we talk to ourselves negatively. Harsh negative self-talk decreases self-respect and self-worth, and it inhibits self assurance and courage. It also leads to depression.

Sometimes we have very high expectations of ourselves. We set high standards that cannot possibly be met. This damages our spirit. Instead, we should begin each day by looking in the mirror and stating three positive attributes about ourselves.

Sometimes we are afraid we have done something so terrible that God will not forgive. Or we spend considerable time feeling guilty about something that happened years ago. God has promised that no sin is so bad that He will not forgive. *"If we confess our sins, he is faithful and just and will forgive us our sins and purify us from all unrighteousness."* (1 John 1:9 NIV) We can have difficulty accepting forgiveness from others, thinking we are not worthy. Not accepting forgiveness from others can lead to spiritual distress. Enjoy today. We need to forgive ourselves so that we can leave our past where it belongs, in the past.

—

Apologize to Others

Sometimes we inadvertently or consciously hurt others. After we see their reaction or think about our words, we realize that we need to apologize. Sometimes we think apologizing is a sign of weakness. It is actually a sign of strength. People respect us when we have the courage to say "I'm sorry."

We may say to ourselves that the information that hurt the individual was accurate. In this instance we need to ask ourselves a question, "What is the highest priority, the idea of being right, or the relationship?"

"Confess your sins to each other and pray for each other so that you may be healed. The earnest prayer of a righteous person has great power and produces wonderful results." (James 5:16 NLT)

A sincere apology does not need a response. It is about the individuals who have hurt others apologizing for their contribution to the situation.

Avoid Bitterness

"Get rid of all bitterness, rage, anger, harsh words, and slander, as well as all types of evil behavior." (Ephesians 4:32 NLT). Bitterness may develop from our inability to forgive another. Bitterness is like when we swallow poison and hope it will hurt someone else. The other person is not affected, but the poison destroys the sole of the bitter person. When bitterness develops we need to talk to God about the situation and ask for His forgiveness for being bitter. We also need to ask God to forgive

30

those who caused our bitterness, just as He forgives us. It is easier for us to forgive others when we know that Jesus gave His life to forgive us.

Don't Blame God

The question, "Why do bad things happen to good people," has been pondered for generations. So many people blame God for problems in their lives, such as natural disasters, death, car accidents and illness. But, bad things happen because we live in a broken world.

Tragedies can happen because of our poor choices. God gave us free will. In other times bad things happen to us because of bad choices by others. A teenager who is killed by a drunk driver is the victim of somebody else's poor decision. That does not mean God caused it. He gives us freedom to make bad choices, but hopes we will choose not to.

The New Testament makes it clear that not everything that happens is God's will. Jesus encouraged His disciples to pray that God's will be done. *"May your kingdom come, may your will be done on earth as it is in heaven."* (Matthew 6:10 ISV) It is not God's will that there be pain and suffering. God wants the best for us. Tragedies such as earthquakes have been with God's children since the beginning of time. When tragedy happens, we need to turn to God for comfort, knowing that with His love and support we can endure anything and eventually be with Him and our loved ones in Heaven.

Avoid Always Seeking Perfection

Expecting life on Earth to be perfect will only frustrate you. We will only be disappointed if we expect others to be perfect. We should not depend on others to provide for us only what Jesus can. He is the only perfect person.

We must watch out for those who promise us the perfect way to lose weight, the perfect mate or the perfect house. Only heaven is perfect. We cannot imagine how perfect heaven will be. *"My Father's house has many rooms; if that were not so, would I have told you that I am going there to prepare a place for you."* (John 14:2 NIV).

Be Kind to Yourself

Sometimes we are so focused on helping others that we neglect ourselves. Treat yourself with at least as much love and caring as you treat others. Support and commend yourself for trying to do your best. Use these positive affirmations, "I am doing my best and that is all I can expect of myself." "Good work." "I am staying focused." "I am doing great." The well-known phrase, "I am my own worst enemy," is very true. *"To acquire wisdom is to love oneself"* (Proverbs 19:8a NLT)

We shouldn't expect perfection of ourselves. Perfectionists equate their self-worth with flawless performance; they dwell on trivial details and devote too much time to projects, which slows productivity. They also cover up errors to maintain a heroic image, and dwell on what's wrong with them or what they didn't accomplish. Instead, we should pay attention to the positive. Sometimes good is good enough.

Just as we become what we think about, we also become what we say to ourselves. The most powerful words we can repeat are, "I like myself." We must refuse to say anything about ourselves that we do not sincerely desire to be true.

Communication with Self and Others

Avoid Negative Thoughts

Turn negative thoughts into positive thoughts. When we allow negative thoughts and feelings to turn over in our mind, we rob our ability to enjoy the day. King David also struggled with negative thoughts. *"How long must I wrestle with my thoughts and day after day have sorrow in my heart? How long will my enemy triumph over me?"* (Psalm 13:2 NIV) We may not have control over certain occurrences in our lives or the actions of others, but we can control our thinking. Pray to God to remove any negative thought and replace with a positive one. Changing the way we perceive circumstances and events can lead to a dramatic change in our experience, even in the worst situations. *"Here on earth you will have many trials and sorrows. But take heart, because I have overcome the world"* (John 16:33b NLT)

Negative thinkers tend to be pessimistic, while positive thinkers are optimistic. People who are optimistic have an attitude that says, "I can achieve this." When we think negative thoughts about ourselves we consider ourselves to be inferior to others, lacking skills, creativity, popularity or intelligence. God has given us many gifts; we just do not always recognize them. Those of us with negative thoughts should consistently strive to replace them with positive thoughts. The negative thought of "I failed" can be replaced with the positive thought of "I made a mistake. I will learn from it and not let it happen again."

We should write positive thoughts and affirmations about ourselves. For example, "I am a great_____!!" Not only should we think positively, we need a plan to fulfill these thoughts. Without a plan, positive thinking can quickly degenerate into positive wishing and positive hoping. We must develop confidence in our abilities. Statements like, "I can't handle this" and "There is no use" can be replaced with, "I can handle this," "I have handled situations like this before and I can handle this too." Our lives are the product of our thoughts. We need to think right to live an abundant life with joy and happiness.

Avoid Negative Communication

Sometimes jealousy will cause us to gossip and say false things to others. *"A perverse person stirs up conflict, and a gossip separates close friends."* (Proverbs 16:28 NIV) If someone says something unkind about us, we should live so that no one will believe it. Those who gossip and backbite are focused on the negative, and can't see the positive.

Control Angry Thoughts

When we are angry, our first thought is to get even. God admonishes us to return good for evil. This won't cause those who have wronged us to necessarily change their ways, but that is what God asks us to do. Jesus said, *"But I say, love your enemies! Pray for those who persecute you!"* (Matthew 5:44 NLT) The only way to get rid of our enemies is to make them our friends.

Don't Worry

Worry can best be defined as a chain of negative thoughts that have to do with fears about the future. Worriers do not feel they have control over things that happen in their lives.

Worriers do not have lives with more traumatic events or stressful situations than non-worriers. Not all people who experience terrible or stressful situations worry. Worrying is just the way some people think.

Worry is like being in a rocking chair. It keeps us very busy, but gets us nowhere. Ask God for help. "Let go and let God." *"Give all your worries to God, because he cares about you."* (1 Peter 5:7 NLT) Give positive uplifting messages to those who ruminate. We cannot change them, but we can be positive role models.

Choose a Good Attitude

"Do everything without grumbling or arguing." (Philippians 2:14 NIV) There are many areas in life over which we have no control. But we can control our attitude. The attitude we choose will determine whether we will have a day filled with joy or one in which others will perceive us as a "grump." *"This is the day that the Lord has made. We will rejoice and be glad in it."* (Psalm 118:24 NLT) A positive attitude is essential for us to cope with difficult times. In good times it is easy to be positive. It is in the down times that maintaining that attitude is difficult. We need to ask God to help us with our attitude, so that we can look for the positive in all situations, ourselves and others.

No matter what is happening in our life, we are to be grateful. Paul admonishes us to be thankful. *"Give thanks in all circumstances, for this is God's will for you in Christ Jesus."* (1 Thessalonians 5:18 NLT) Thank God for all your blessings. Even on days when nothing seems to be going right, we can thank God that things are not worse. We can thank God for being there to listen to us. We can thank God for the great day we had yesterday, a friend or a warm place to sleep. Focusing on being thankful can change the quality of our day.

Understand Happiness vs. Joy

The word "joy" comes from a Greek word meaning to be exceedingly glad. *"Consider it pure joy, my brothers and sisters whenever you face trials of many kinds."* (James 1:2 NIV) True joy is everlasting and not dependent upon circumstances. Philippians, written while the Apostle Paul was imprisoned in Rome, teaches us how to have true contentment in Jesus Christ, despite our circumstances.

The Bible teaches that happiness is fleeting because it often depends on things outside of us. Sometimes we think it is the responsibility of others to make us happy, but that is our own decision. Depending on others to make us happy will only frustrate us and leave us upset with those we love. Being happy does not mean everything is perfect. It means we have decided to look beyond the imperfection of our lives.

Healthy Living

Healthy Lifestyle Choices

Developing a healthy lifestyle may seem simple, but implementing consistent long-term changes is challenging. The Bible admonishes us to care for our bodies. *"After all, no one ever hated their own body, but they feed and care for it, just as Christ does the church."* (Ephesians 5:29 NIV)

The following steps lead to success:

- Exercise. It is essential for a healthy lifestyle, relieves muscle tension and improves mental health. We should choose the exercise we enjoy and develop a plan to do it regularly.
- Eat healthy balanced meals. Healthy food has a positive influence on our health, physical performance and state of mind.
- Avoid beverages high in sugar and caffeine. Eight glasses of water per day can actually help reduce fatigue.
- Expose yourself to sunlight every day. Sunlight not only supplies Vitamin D, it also eases depression.
- Get adequate sleep. Sleep is essential to the body, and while we all require different amounts, on average aim to sleep about 8 hours a night. Sleep can be affected in stressful times. This can be caused by preoccupation with a difficult situation. It is important to break the chain of stressful thoughts at least 30 minutes before going to bed. Try relaxing, listening to music or reading.

Manage Stress

None of us can avoid stress. It happens when we are tired, in a new environment, not feeling good, worried about our security or when we have taken on more than we can handle.

- Assess what is causing the stress. Ask yourself, "What's going on?" "What is wrong?" "How am I going to approach it?" "What is it that needs to be done in order to handle this?" "Do I need to get help?

- Set aside time to pray and read the Bible daily. Remember that God is with you always. *"Even though I walk through the Valley of the shadow of death, I will fear no evil, for you are with me; your rod and your staff, they comfort me.* (Psalm 24:3 NIV) Note in this verse that God walks us through the valley. He does not leave us there.

- Schedule time alone to meditate, to sit in nature, read an inspiring book, or listen to music. *"Cast all anxiety on him because he cares for you."* (1 Peter 5:7 NIV)

- Relieve tension by learning to relax in difficult situations. Take a few minutes to take slow deep breaths. Even a few minutes of deep breathing will produce noticeable changes in tension levels. Deep breathing can be done several times a day in many settings. Taking several deep breaths just before, during and after a stressful situation is calming and increases feelings of control.

- Get active! Exercise is probably the best stress-reliever.

- Let your self-talk be positive! If we tell ourselves we cannot handle a situation we only compound the problem. Replace all negative statements with powerful positive statements such as "I handled difficult situations before. I can handle this too." "I can't take this stress," "I feel like I will boil over," "I need chocolate," can be replaced with the positive thought "I'll go for a walk at lunch and listen to some relaxing music, and then it will be easier to handle this situation."

- Watch what you eat. Eating high calorie foods such as chips and brownies will just make you feel worse and less able to cope.
- Seek support of family and our Best Friend, Jesus.
- Seek support of positive friends. Asking a friend whom you respect for input can provide a different perspective. A hug from a friend can also be very therapeutic.
- Journal. Keep a daily record of feelings, occurrences, experiences, or observations. Whether it is written words or drawing journaling allows us to discover more about ourselves.
- Use imagery. Tension can be lowered quite rapidly by taking a few deep breaths and imagining a pleasant scene. A pleasant scene can be anything positive and a special place we can visit at any time and in any situation to relax and refuel. Just a three-to-four minute visit will have a rejuvenating effect.
- Add humor. It will eliminate a good deal of the negative stress.

Enjoy Humor

Humor is not only enjoyable, but also one of the best antidotes to stress. It gives people a different perspective on stressful situations. *"He will yet fill your mouth with laughter and your lips with shouts of joy."* (Job 8:21 NIV) Keeping our sense of humor, even in the midst of chaos, helps us regain control, if not over the situation, at least of our response.   Laughter is not a way to avoid our problems or deny the seriousness of the situation. But it can be a way to release stress and balance distress with positive feelings.   Seeing the positive helps keep our troubles in perspective and can even help us find positive solutions to problems.

Living a Christian Lifestyle

Choose the Right Relationships and Friends

It is important that throughout life we make the right relationship choices. Some may seem like they would be fun, but will actually lead us astray. We may later regret a quick decision to follow the crowd or someone who makes destructive choices.

The most important relationship we will ever develop is with God. Comfort can be found in this text, *"When you pass through the waters, I will be with you; and when you pass through the rivers, they will not sweep over you. When you walk through the fire, you will not be burned; the flames will not set you ablaze."* (Isaiah 43:2 NIV)

Many of us believe that confiding in others and talking out our problems can be a helpful way to get good advice or uncritical support. When we feel like yelling, or sense depression coming on, we need to call someone to help us regain our sense of balance. But most of all, we need to talk to our Best Friend, God. Remember that He is available to talk 24 hours a day.

Embrace God's Grace

Grace is God's good news for us. It is God's unmerited favor. We are not saved by good works, or by our efforts or merits. It's only by grace. God's grace is given to us for our benefit, because

He loves us. We are saved because Jesus died on the cross. He died in our place. There is nothing we can do to earn this. It is totally free. *"For it is by grace you have been saved through faith – and this is not from yourself, it is a gift from God."* (Ephesians 2:8 NIV)

Spending eternity with Jesus has nothing to do with our past or how good we are. Our salvation is not prohibited by how sinful we have been. Jesus came into the world to save sinners. We are never too sinful to be saved, but we may be too self-righteous or self-sufficient to accept salvation.

"Intoxicated with unbroken success, we have become too self sufficient to feel the necessity of redeeming and preserving grace, too proud to pray to the God that made us." ~ Abraham Lincoln

Be Assured of God's Love

Life comes with burdens and overwhelming situations. We can feel all alone and that no one cares or loves us. We must be assured that God cares. *"Cast all your anxiety on him because he cares for you."* (1 Peter 5:7 NIV) God knows what we are facing and He cares. His love for each one of his children is immeasurable. It is greater than love from anyone on Earth. He has compassion on our every pain, every crisis, and every struggle in life. *"As a father has compassion on his children, so the Lord has compassion on those who fear Him!"* (Psalms 103:13 NIV) God is our Father and He cares and loves us.

Know That Jesus is Alive

Where do you envision Jesus? Sometimes we see Him in a manger, tomb or in the Bible. Jesus is indeed there, but more importantly He is with us, walking beside us, each and every day. A verse from the hymn, "In the Garden," reads, "He walks with me and He talks with me and tells me I am his own." *"And surely I am with you always, to the very end of the age."* (Matthew 28:20b NIV)

Trust in God

Some of us have tried to solve a problem when we had no insight on to how to do it. Or we have tried to accomplish something or worked endlessly to reach a goal. Finally, when nothing is accomplished we turn to God saying, "It is in God's hands." When we have problems and concerns we need to right away give them to God and trust Him to solve them. How often have we gone through trials only to look back and realize that we would never have believed it would work out so well? When we give our concerns to God immediately instead of after we fail, we will feel a huge relief. *"Lean on, trust in, and be confident in the Lord with all your heart and mind and do not rely on your own insight or understanding."* (Proverbs 3:5 AMP)

Have Faith

Faith is the complete and unquestioning acceptance of God that cannot be proven by logical thought. Faith is the bird that sings when the dawn is still dark or knowing that spring is just around the corner on a March blizzard. Faith gives life meaning, providing us with strength in times of difficulty. All difficulties in life are eased when we have faith. *"I have fought the good fight, I have finished the race, I have kept the faith."* (2 Timothy 4:7 NIV) We need to use our faith in Jesus in every situation that causes us distress. Having faith takes effort. Faith grows within our hearts, as we walk with Him and talk with Him, we nurture our faith. Faith will grow as we spend time with God. Like anything worth having, we must work to attain faith and work to keep it.

It is one thing to believe we have faith. It is another thing to mobilize that faith and practice it. Out of practicing faith we develop a new confidence and peace.

Know That Jesus is the Way
Today we are asked to be tolerant. Tolerance is admirable. We are tolerant of the cultures of others and their ways of life. Jesus, too, was tolerant. But Jesus said there was only one way to salvation. *"I am the way, the truth, and the life. No one can come to the father except through me."* (John 14:6 NLT)

Jesus did not think there were several ways to get to the Father. According to Him, there are not several options; the only way to the Father is through Him.

Have Hope

Because we have faith, we can have Hope. Faith is the belief in God, whereas hope is the belief that things will get better. Without hope we are hopeless and helpless and in spiritual distress. When we feel down, discouraged or lonely, we need to remember that happiness will ultimately come back, that its absence will never be permanent.

Hope gives us the courage to get up each morning with a grateful heart. This is the time to remember positive events that have occurred in the past and look forward to God's blessings in the future. We all need to make a decision to have hope. Thinking positively will help rejuvenate our ability to hope.

The ability to hope for something better enables us to cope with fears and uncertainty. In Romans, the Apostle Paul writes, *"Let your hope keep you joyful, be patient in your troubles and pray at all times"*(Romans 12:12 GNB) Hope keeps us from falling into discouragement because we know their will always be another tomorrow and at last heaven.

Confident people have hope because they believe that life is good and see positive outcomes for the future. Hopeful people don't necessarily have wonderful circumstances but because they have hope, their life appears to be great.

When you feel overwhelmed with the problems/challenges of life, it helps to remember the words of the psalm, *"Weeping may last through the night, but joy comes with the morning."* (Psalm 30:5b NLT) We all need hope. We must rise above the tough times and persevere, knowing that better times will come.

Use Meditation

Meditation quiets the mind and focuses our thoughts to release worries, fears, anxieties and doubts of the present and the past. Jesus does not use the word meditation, but initiated the disciples into the value of time apart from their busy active ministry. He invited them to have quality time with Him. *"Let's get away from the crowds for a while and rest."* (Mark 6:31 NLT) The purpose of meditation is "to be still and know that God is God." He wants us to engage in mediation and spend time "quietly thinking about God, feeling the presence of God, trying to listen to God speaking, and worshiping and adoring God."

Most of us would like to take time to meditate, but do not give it a priority in our busy schedules. We feel guilty or do not feel it is a priority or are too distracted to spend time meditating and listening to the Spirit. When we don't, we are depriving ourselves of a relationship with God, who wants to renew our spirit.

There are many types of meditation, but focusing attention and relaxation are important components of all of them. These guidelines can assist in meditation:

- Location. A quiet place in the presence of silence is essential in order to think deep thoughts. We need to find a special place that we love. It may be a favorite chair, a hammock in the backyard, or a place in nature. It is essential that it is a quiet comfortable place away from distractions.

- Time. Ideally the morning or the evening are best for meditation, but setting a specific time for meditation is important This can take as little as 10 minutes per day.
- Breathing. Taking some slow deep breaths calms our mind. This allows us to slow our bodies, clear our minds and brings clarity to our thoughts. Breathing allows us to relax.
- Listening. Practicing meditation is developing "inner listening skills." This is not a time to judge our thoughts or tell ourselves what we should have done differently. It is a time to take an inner journey to our soul.

We should come from meditation feeling renewed. *"I will refresh the weary and satisfy the faint."* (Jeremiah 31:25 NIV) Meditation enables us to have a feeling of greater spiritual wellbeing and wholeness. Refreshing our soul will refresh our spirit. The goal is aimed at finding serenity in our lives and being at peace and harmony with ourselves and the world around us.

Embrace Prayer

Prayer is communicating with God in word and thought. It is simply "talking with God." It is a tool for seeking God's help. We can talk to God because He is always listening. He takes us very seriously. We are never ignored, even if our words are not polished. God is impressed with your words even if others are not.

Jesus took time to pray. *"Now it was in those days that Jesus went to a mountain to pray, and he spent the whole night in prayer to God."* (Luke 6:12 ISV) Caring for our spirit requires pausing and taking time to pray. God does wonderful things in our lives. Many of these are in response to our prayers. Unfortunately, many individuals do not pray as a first resort, instead only when nothing else works. In all matters we need to seek His guidance, yielding to Him, and listening for His direction.

Jesus encouraged us to pray constantly. God wants to hear all our concerns. There are many types of prayer and many ways of praying:

- Giving honor and praise to God. He is righteous, holy powerful, and in all places we need to acknowledge Him for that. He is the Good Shepherd who cares for us. God deserves our praise.
- Thanking God for his goodness. Thanksgiving is a holiday in which we offer prayers of thanks to God. We need to let God know how much we appreciate the little and big things He does for us each day. In all situations, good and bad, we should thank God.
- Asking for something for ourselves. Whatever we need, great or small, share it with God. We need to ask for what we need, be it food, clothes, forgiveness, peace of mind, or a purpose in life. For all these things we need to talk to God.

- Praying for others. There is great power in prayer, and praying for our friends in time of need is the most important thing we can do for them. It is also important to pray for those we do not know. Those who are rude and insulting can use our prayers because obviously they are very distraught.
- Seeking forgiveness for wrongdoing. God promises forgiveness of sins for those who ask. All guilt is removed when God forgives sins.
- Requesting guidance. We need to pray for guidance on small matters as well as when we have a crisis in our lives. In all matters we need to seek His guidance, yielding to Him, and listening for his direction.
- Talking with our Best Friend. This is a reason that we frequently do not consider. Many of us grew up having a very formal relationship with God or no relationship at all. But if God is our friend, then he should be someone we can communicate with at any time and about everything. We should take God in prayer with us everywhere, to work, school, and even when we are doing mundane tasks such as laundry or cleaning. If we do this we will be doing what Jesus requested. *"Be unceasing in prayer."* (1 Thessalonians 5:17 AMP)
- Connecting people to God, and to the power available to intervene. There are no perfect words, ways or places to pray. It is not the words we say that contributes to our wellbeing. It is the extent and depth of intimacy with God, our Best Friend, that most contributes to our spiritual wellness.

When we pray we experience a positive effect on our mental health and keep spiritually fit.

Remember the Holy Spirit

The Trinity can be difficult to understand. Most of us can grasp the Father and Son, but the Spirit is vague. The Holy Spirit is the presence of God in our lives. He is doing the work of Jesus. The Holy Spirit prays for us and fills our lives with God's love. *"For all who are led by the Spirit of God are children of God."* (Romans 8:14 NLT) The Spirit should be a great comfort to us.

God the Holy Spirit is not dormant within us. He is in us to bring us to do God's purpose on Earth. "Fruit of the Spirit" is a biblical term that sums up nine visible characteristics of a true Christian life. Apostle Paul in his letter to the Galatians lists these nine "fruit." *"But the fruit of the Spirit is love, joy, peace, forbearance, kindness, goodness, faithfulness, gentleness and self-control."* (Galatians 5:22-23 NIV) These fruit are what God wants each of us to have in our personalities. These fruit have the ability to change us and in turn to affect the lives of those around us.

Following Jesus

Care about the World's Problems

"Love your neighbor as yourself. No other commandment is greater than these." (Mark 12:31 NLT) Jesus was concerned about people and the situations in which they lived. We are not to isolate ourselves from our communities and world. Instead, we must share in their difficulties and problems. We must feed the hungry and assist the homeless. God loves all people. And just as He was compassionate, we must be compassionate, too. *"When he saw the crowds, he had compassion on them."* (Matthew 9:36 NIV) The world needs people to make a difference. It is good for us to help others, because is almost impossible to be depressed or discouraged when we are helping others.

Be Compassionate

God is compassionate to us. He suffers with all of us and admonishes us to have compassion on others, to suffer with them. We must reach out to those less fortunate than ourselves, by visiting the elderly or assisting the homeless. *"Live in harmony with one another; be sympathetic, love as brothers, be compassionate and humble."* (1 Peter 3:8 NIV)

Make Caring a Way of Life

A positive caring attitude is much more attractive than beauty or nice clothes. We are admonished throughout the Bible to care for one another. *"Let your light shine before men, that they may see your*

good deeds and praise your Father in heaven."
(Matthew 5:16 NIV) We are encouraged to
develop a spirituality of action. "*We are God's
fellow workers.*" (1Corinthians 3:9 NIV)
Maintaining our spirituality means we care for
others.

Albert Einstein once reflected on the purpose of
man's existence:

> Strange is our situation here upon Earth.
> Each of us comes for a short visit, not
> knowing why, yet sometimes seeming to a
> divine purpose. From the standpoint of
> daily life, however, there is one thing we
> do know. That we are here for the sake of
> others...for the countless unknown souls
> with whose fate we are connected by a
> bond of sympathy. Many times a day, I
> realize how much my own outer and inner
> life is built upon the labors of people, both
> living and dead, and how earnestly I must
> exert myself in order to give in return as I
> have received.

Caring about another elevates us to a level beyond
ourselves. Doing something for another will lessen
our spiritual distress and lift our spirits. There are
many opportunities we can offer a helping hand to
others, including:

- Random Acts of Kindness. When our day
  couldn't get any worse and we're feeling
  down, a friend, complete stranger or family
  member's act of kindness can change our
  day. We, too, can reach out to others
  through random acts of kindness. Be alert

for individuals who would benefit from random acts of kindness. Holding the door or offering our seat for someone who is older or handicapped will lighten their load. Never underestimate the importance of these random acts of kindness.

- Good Deeds. Life satisfaction increases and depression decreases when we regularly volunteer. Caring for others forces us away from being focused on our troubles.

- Kind Words. Helping to heal another heals our hearts as well. Kind words should be conveyed with warmth and sincerity and with eye contact and a gentle voice. Giving a compliment or telling others they did a great job will brighten their day. Some people rarely hear positive comments, so bringing kindness into the lives of others gives us energy, increases our self-esteem, and provides a feeling of personal empowerment.

Remember, we were created for good works. *"We are God's handiwork, created in Christ Jesus for the good works God prepared in advance for us to do."* (Ephesians 2:10 NIV).

We should also notice the many times people reach out to us in a helpful way. The opportunities to contribute to another's life are unending. When we block ourselves off from others we are vulnerable to spiritual distress. To maintain our spirituality we need to care about the dreams and sorrows of others. We need to listen intently with our ears, see with our eyes, and reach out with our arms to hug those in need of comfort.

Eleanor Roosevelt personifies caring when she said, "When you cease to make a contribution you begin to die." When we close ourselves off from others and do not care, we have destroyed the vital contribution we need to make to receive and maintain our spirituality. Caring is love in action and love in action promotes spiritual health in others and ultimately ourselves.

Conclusion

All Christians have to deal with traumatic events such as death, broken relationships, lost careers and heartbreak. As Christians we are not promised the opportunity to go through life trouble free.

Life seldom turns out the way that we imagined it would, and we need to accept it with grace and continually strive to do our best to contribute and develop the gifts that God has given us.

We can follow these guidelines and refer to the verses from the Bible to help us through whatever challenge we are facing.

Our goal in life should be to develop and maintain a lifestyle and attitude pleasing to God. This requires that each day we strive to come closer to living a life that He would want us to live. In so doing we have a fulfilled life that will enable us to be happier and healthier. God has offered us a wonderful life greater than we ever dreamed possible; each day strive to work toward this goal.

Scripture References

NOTES, IDEAS & PLANS

13530833R00033

Made in the USA
Charleston, SC
16 July 2012